MAGNETS

A Buddy Book

by

Julie Murray

ABDO
Publishing Company

VISIT US AT
www.abdopublishing.com

Published by ABDO Publishing Company, 4940 Viking Drive, Edina, Minnesota 55435.

Copyright © 2007 by Abdo Consulting Group, Inc. International copyrights reserved in all countries. No part of this book may be reproduced in any form without written permission from the publisher. Buddy Books™ is a trademark and logo of ABDO Publishing Company.

Printed in the United States.

Series Coordinator: Sarah Tieck
Contributing Editor: Michael P. Goecke
Graphic Design: Maria Hosley
Cover Photograph: Media Bakery
Interior Photographs/Illustrations: Media Bakery, Photos.com

Library of Congress Cataloging-in-Publication Data

Murray, Julie, 1969–
    Magnets / Julie Murray.
       p. cm. — (First science)
    Includes bibliographical references and index.
    ISBN-13: 978-1-59679-827-4
    ISBN-10: 1-59679-827-0
    1. Magnets—Juvenile literature. 2. Magnetism—Juvenile literature. I. Title. II. Series: Murray, Julie, 1969- First Science.

QC757.5.M87 2007
538'.4—dc22

                                              2006013329

TABLE OF CONTENTS

A MAGNETIC WORLD

Magnets are part of our everyday life. It is easy to see them in action in many places. Just look around!

Magnets stick to surfaces. They help fasten objects together. Also, magnets help make some machines work.

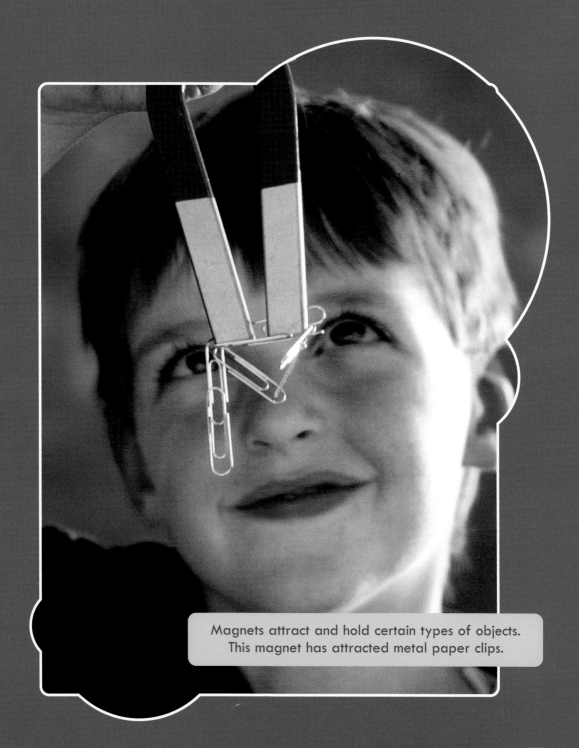

Magnets attract and hold certain types of objects.
This magnet has attracted metal paper clips.

THE SCIENCE OF MAGNETS

To understand magnets, you must understand **force**. Forces make things move by pushing or pulling. Force can't be seen with the eye. But, force can be experienced.

Magnets put out a force. That force either pushes things apart or pulls them together.

Magnets are used in everyday places such as offices. This container has a magnet that holds paper clips within reach.

MAGNETIC POLES

Magnetic **force** can **attract** things. This is why a magnet sticks to a steel school locker.

High-speed trains use magnets to help reduce the friction of the train on the tracks. This allows the train to move faster.

Magnetic **force** can also **repel** things. This is what helps make high-speed trains work.

Magnets **attract** and repel because they have **poles**. There are usually two poles. One is called the north pole. The other is called the south pole. These poles are opposites.

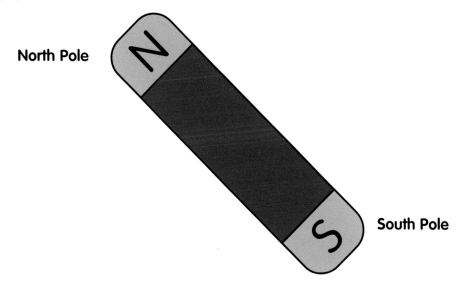

North Pole

South Pole

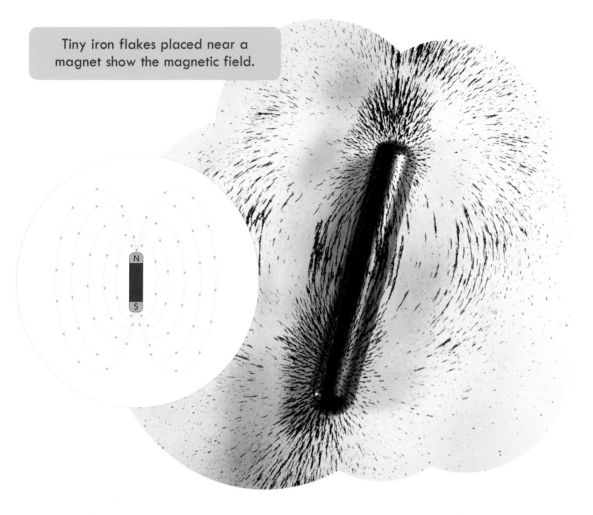

When you put two magnets together, opposite **poles attract**. Poles that are the same **repel** each other.

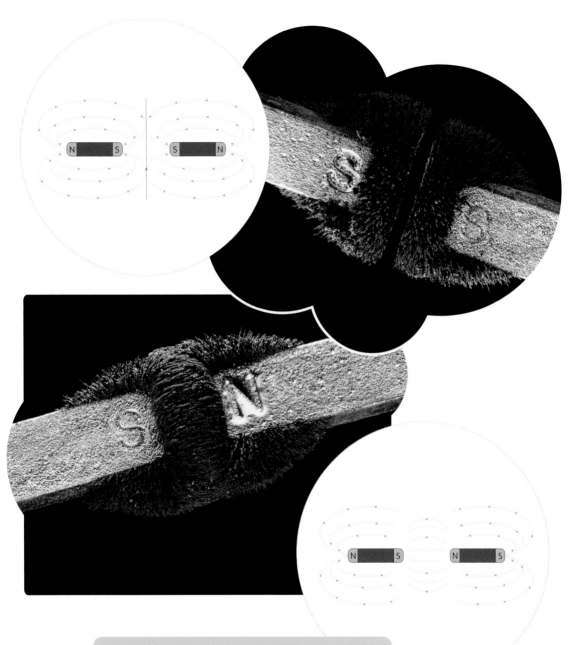

These iron flakes show how like poles repel
(top) and opposite poles attract (bottom).

HOW MAGNETS WORK

Magnets will not stick to all surfaces. For instance, a magnet will not stick to an orange or the family dog.

Magnets are **attracted** to certain metals, such as iron and steel. That is why magnets stick to refrigerators.

These refrigerator magnets are examples of man-made magnets.

Most magnets are man-made. But, some magnets are natural. The **mineral** magnetite is a natural magnet. It is a weak magnet.

Some man-made magnets are in the shape of a "U". In this shape, the magnet's north and south poles are next to each other.

N   S

Some objects can become magnetic if they are placed near magnets. If a screw is placed on a magnet, it can become magnetic. When this happens, another screw can stick to the first one.

Sometimes, doctors use magnets to help people get better. The Magnetic Resonance Imaging (MRI) scanning machine helps doctors.

The MRI machine has very strong magnets. These magnets allow the machine to take detailed pictures of the inside of a person's body. This helps doctors treat their patients.

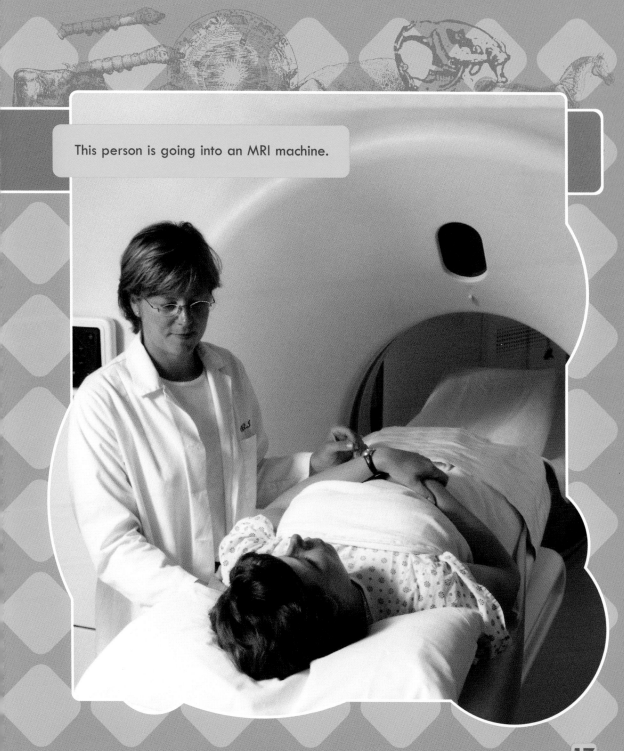

This person is going into an MRI machine.

PULLED THROUGH HISTORY

Through the years many scientists have tried to understand the science of magnets. One of these scientists was a man named William Gilbert. He was the doctor for Queen Elizabeth I of England.

In 1600, Gilbert studied magnets. Gilbert was one of the first to talk about magnets and **poles**. He said that Earth is a magnet.

North Pole

South Pole

The Earth is a large magnet.

Hans Christian Oersted of Denmark also studied magnets. In 1820, he proved the connection between **electricity** and magnetism. He did this by experimenting with a compass.

Since these experiments, many people have studied magnets. They've made important discoveries about magnets. Still, most agree there is still more to learn about this science.

North Pole

South Pole

The needle of a compass is a magnet.
It points to the Earth's North Pole.

MAGNETS IN THE WORLD TODAY

Magnets help make our lives easier. Without magnets, people wouldn't have batteries. Without magnets, the motors in electrical tools, such as drills, wouldn't work. And, without magnets, no one could use a compass.

The world would be a very different place if there were no magnets.

IMPORTANT WORDS

attract to pull closer.

electricity a form of energy. It is caused by movement of the positive and negative charges in things. Electricity provides power to operate things such as lamps.

force a push or pull against resistance.

mineral a natural substance that was formed in the Earth.

pole either end of the imaginary line that goes through an object. Each end of the line is an opposite.

repel to push away.

WEB SITES

To learn more about **Magnets**, visit ABDO Publishing Company on the World Wide Web. Web site links about **Magnets** are featured on our Book Links page. These links are routinely monitored and updated to provide the most current information available.

www.abdopublishing.com

INDEX